FIXING CHURCH 7.0

A Seven Week Study

BILL KEMP

Print ISBN 13: 978-0-9997687-0-9

Ebook ISBN 13: 978-0-9997687-1-6

All scripture quoted is from the **New International Bible** (NIV®) copyright held by **Biblica** – The International Bible Society, under the fair use agreement displayed on their website. Readers will want to check out the free online version of the NIV® (www.biblegateway.com).

Fixing Church 7.0: A Seven Week Study. Copyright © 2017 **Not Perfect Yet Publishing**. All rights reserved, except as noted by a fair use extended agreement granted by the author, as follows:

1) Portions up to 250 words (about a page) may be used with proper attribution.

2) Churches may make copies of individual chapters and the discussion questions to provide for those that attend their small group discussions.

3) Cover and other images may be copied for one time use and projected for group viewing. Contact bill@notperfectyet.com for any additional use.

Note that our website: www.notperfectyet.com provides additional help in obtaining supplemental material relating to Fixing Church 7.0. Most of Bill Kemp's books were developed in conjunction with his workshops. We hope over 2018 to place the handouts, slide presentations, and other resources for each workshop on this website.

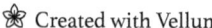 Created with Vellum

CONTENTS

Dedication:	v
- Preface -	vii
1. Begin Here	1
2. Being Passionate	9
3. Being Compassionate	15
4. Being a Fellowship	23
5. Being Worship-filled	33
6. Being Biblical	41
7. Being Church (Soul)	49
About the Author & His Books	57
Also by Bill Kemp:	59

DEDICATION:

For my mother, Mildred Kemp, who never thought that her children needed fixing.

BECAUSE WORDS MATTER:

I am committed to extending the use of gender neutral language in our society. The Church is a better place when we are both progressive and respectful in our speech.

This book has three exceptions:

- Direct quotations (NIV Bible requires the use of their language)
- God is given capitalized male pronouns, even though genderless.
- The Church is given female pronouns, to reflect scripture and tradition.

Even though I am United Methodist, I have limited my use of jargon and have sought to write a book that will be helpful to the lovers of Church in any denomination.

- Bill

- PREFACE -

"We are going to have Church today!" I am in a small, mostly African-American congregation and the worship leader has begun the service. I can hear the capital "C" in his pronunciation of the word *Church*. In this humble sanctuary, even the word *Church* is something to rejoice in. But *Church* doesn't just happen on Sunday. Later in the week, the church council has a tough decision to make. The pastor says, "We need to be the *Church* in this situation." What does she mean? Usually, the word "church" doesn't deserve to be capitalized. Often our church makes us anxious. We wonder how its bills are going to be paid. We whisper, "Do we need a new pastor?" or "Why aren't there more young couples attending our services?" This seven-week series, "Fixing Church 7.0," is all about discovering what you need to have *Church*.

Jesus says,*"When two or three gather in my name, I am with them"* (Matthew 18:20). This is often used to justify small congregations or poorly attended worship services. Read Jesus in context, however, and you will discover his great enthusiasm and expectations for his people whenever and wherever they gather for prayer, fellowship, and service to others. The number of people in the room doesn't matter. What matters for *Church* will be the subject of this study. To be brief, the answer involves transforming people's lives. Our church becomes an albatross around our neck when it stops transforming our lives, and the lives of our neighbors, for the better.

That said, don't think of fixing church in the same way you think of fixing your car or, worse yet, your cat. Think instead of how a radar can fix the location of a ship that is lost in the fog. When I used to develop black and white film (yes, I am that old), the last chemical bath was called "Fixer," for it fixed the image permanently to the photo paper. Jesus wishes to do lasting good through your church. When you become a place for "fixing" his love in your community, then you become *Church* with a capital "C."

Fixing Church is a short course in thinking differently. It doesn't offer quick fixes to your budget. Instead, it asks difficult questions that can reframe the way your fellowship deals with money. It won't help you decide what color to paint the walls. Instead, it will challenge the whole way you think about your church building. You may be hoping that this study will help you get more people into your church. I hate to disappoint you. **Fixing Church** seeks instead to bless people with a *Church* that fixes their lives. It is more concerned with church health than church growth. Above all, it seeks to uncover what Jesus wants from us as we do *Church*.

Fixing Church is an appropriate study for Lent because it provides insight into why Jesus was so passionate about his *Church*. He died, not just for our individual soul, but also for the fellowships that would meet in his name. This study has seven sessions, so you will want to start the week before Lent begins, to reserve Holy Week for the Passion narrative.

Alternatively, you may want to use **Fixing Church** in the Fall, before your church's stewardship drive or annual meeting. However you use this series, note that the final lesson is on simply *Being Church* and deals with matters of the soul. It is appropriate for a more informal setting, say a potluck supper, where you invite spouses and people who haven't been a part of the previous discussions.

Each chapter ends with a short discussion starter. There are also links to appropriate articles in my *Weekly Word* and *Fixing Church* blogs at billkemp.info. A list of topics, providing links to over four years of articles, is found on the left side of each blog's homepage. Pastors will want to note that a sermon starter for the upcoming week is provided each Tuesday and at the Weekly Word tab of the blog. All of my books and other resources can be found on www.notperfectyet.com or at Amazon: Bill Kemp, Author's Page.

Finally, be sure and sign up for my e-letter for promotions and advance offerings. You can also leave a comment or send your review to contact@billkemp.info

EBOOK READERS HAVE THE FOLLOWING QUICK LINKS:

For comments using an **Airtable** *survey.*

For e-letter signup through **MailChimp**.

BEGIN HERE

Jesus begins here:

> *Blessed are the poor in spirit,*
> *for theirs is the kingdom of heaven.*
> *Blessed are those who mourn,*
> *for they will be comforted.*
> *Blessed are the meek,*
> *for they will inherit the earth.*
> *Blessed are those who hunger and thirst for righteousness,*
> *for they will be filled.*
> *Blessed are the merciful,*
> *for they will be shown mercy.*
> *Blessed are the pure in heart,*
> *for they will see God.*
> *Blessed are the peacemakers,*
> *for they will be called children of God...*
> - Matthew 5:3-9

This is literally where Jesus began Church (with a capital 'C'). This is where he invited people into a lively, organic, always learning fellowship. This is also where you begin the next seven weeks. We know this passage as the Beatitudes, or Blessings. They are like a call to worship for Church. Imagine this group of ordinary people gathering on a hillside — it's a beautiful summer day on the shores of the lake — with their kids and perhaps a picnic lunch. Some of them have come because they have a specific need. Perhaps it is an incurable illness or a troubling emotional ache. They have heard things about Jesus; some may even know a lot about him. They are not too different from the people who gather at your church. Jesus has something to say to everyone gathered. I imagine him repeating these blessings everywhere he went.

There are two kinds of people on that hillside and in your church: Broken people who need to know that they are blessed, and Blessed people who need to share the blessings of Jesus with others. Many people, perhaps most, fall into both camps. You may find it helpful to see yourself coming some weeks as a broken person, and other weeks as someone who wants to learn how to be a blessing. The two tasks, healing brokenness and expressing one's gratitude through actively being a blessing, complement each other. This was the genius of Jesus' design for Church. We call the work of learning how to bless others as Jesus blessed us, discipleship. We call the work of inviting broken people to know our Jesus, evangelism (literally sharing the Good News). Sometimes, we send these blessings beyond our church walls and call it missions (from *to be sent*).

Discuss the following quote:

> *The Church exists by mission, just as a fire exists by burning.*
> - Emil Brunner

THE GOAL JESUS HAS FOR US IS NOT TO GET MORE PEOPLE INTO church, but to get the blessings of Church out into the lives of people. We often divide our church work into two opposing camps; committees and projects that deal with our local church and keeping our doors open, and committees that deal with missions and evangelism. Whenever we have a meeting, no matter what the stated purpose is, some members will need to be blessed, and some will need to practice discipleship. This is item one on the agenda. Discipleship, missions, evangelism, membership care, and Jesus-like blessing is the work of the whole church, not just certain committees. The average church building is capable of out-lasting our faith. The average church committee, however, might continue meeting and keeping busy long after everyone has forgotten how to bless others.

Where do you see God active in your community? Can you name an event or a place where one of the blessings named above is being shared? Where have you seen the broken receiving healing? Are those who mourn being comforted? Does your church help the oppressed to receive justice? Do you run away from the conflicts that surround you, or are you intentional about making peace? If you want to be in mission, then you need to look for where God is acting and find some way to partner with Him. If you want to be a disciple of Jesus, then learn how to bless others.

With this in mind, avoid thinking of Christians as being on different levels. It is impossible for one person to be more important than another if we all equally hear Jesus speaking his beatitudes to us. A saint is not a person who dies as a martyr for the faith; neither is it a person who is always working in church. We are all saints as we receive and share God's blessings.

Each of Jesus' blessings is a reversal in our definition of

"saint." Those with impoverished faith (poor in spirit) are sanctified. The religious leaders with their "rich" theological traditions are shut out of God's kingdom. The meek are praised and the ambitious considered un-saintly. Mourning counts for something. The bad theology that considers our misfortunes to be punishments for being less than perfect, is thrown in the trash bin. The messy and politically unappreciated work of peace-making is prized.

Our default setting (or culture) is to bless the ambitious, the financially savvy, the lucky, the young, and the beautiful. For Jesus' people sainthood involves purity of heart. What if we turn to those who mourn and ask them for their wisdom? What if we honor peace makers as the real heroes of our society? What if we bless and pray with those who are honest about their spiritual poverty? Then, we might begin to have Church.

DR SEUSS WROTE SEVERAL CHILDREN'S BOOKS ABOUT THE importance of everyone having a voice. In one, *The Lorax,* an evil industrialist is chopping down all the *truffula trees* and making them into *thneeds*. Trees don't have a voice, so Dr Seuss has someone speak for them:"I am the Lorax, I speak for the trees." Although this line is stated repeatedly, no one listens; soon, all the trees are gone. Only one seed remains. The book is not simply an environmental parable, but also an appeal for us to be advocates for those whom we see being broken around us.

The more I read Jesus, especially the blessings above, the more I see them as his definition of sainthood. Matthew 5:3-13 should be the credo of every local church. With both Dr Seuss and Jesus in mind, I offer the following:

I am today's Christian, representing the Kingdom of God:

*I speak for the poor — for everything belongs to them.
I speak for those that mourn — that my church might hear about them, pray for them, and comfort them.
I speak for the meek — for they are defined by their lack of voice.
Instead of judging others, I will strive to be pure in my own heart — for the Devil knows my price.
I will also speak for those that hunger for justice — for many of our church's neighbors have given up on the system.
In doing this I will work to make the church more merciful — for we receive mercy only by sharing it.
Similarly, I will work for peace — for the cost of hatred is too great.
Further, I will stand with all those who are persecuted, insulted, and shut out of our nation's political discourse
— For when joined with them I am the salt of the earth.
I am a Christian and I will not be silent.*

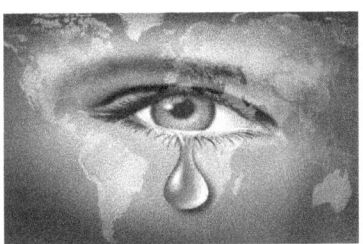

For more:
www.billkemp.info/tags/beatitudes

FOR DISCUSSION

Discuss each of these questions. Then, see what Bill says. What insights did you have that Bill missed?
Be sure and talk about both what you are currently doing and what might be good for the future.

1) Talk about the word "blessing." Where do you need it? How do you share blessings?

2) What would Jesus preach if he were in your church's pulpit this Sunday? Don't just say "love." Be specific.

3) What is your definition of a saint?

BILL'S THOUGHTS:

1) We all need to be assured that we are okay. Jesus says when we are broken, "Look, here and now, God loves you and has your best interests in His heart." When we bless others, it often takes more than just words. We must be willing to show up, work alongside those in need, and by our presence, give hope to the afflicted.

2) I think Jesus starts every sermon the same way, blessing those who need it. Then he teaches specific lessons about life skills, such as turning the other cheek (forgiveness) and living

simply ("consider the lilies of the field" - Matthew 6:28). He might also teach your congregation how to be a better blessing to those outside your church walls.

3) THE WORD "SAINT" MEANS A PERSON WHO IS SET APART FOR holy work (sanctified). All of us have been set apart for holy work. We are already saints; we just have to let our outside activities catch up with our inner blessings.

2
BEING PASSIONATE

At McDonald's, we get asked if we want to supersize our order. It doesn't cost much more. Unfortunately, there isn't a fast food restaurant, or a church, that will deliver super-sized Christianity. If we could super-size our faith, what would that look like? If you had a church whose intention was to increase the portion of each member's spiritual passion, how would that be different from the way your church is now?

The mid-section of Luke, from the Transfiguration (Luke 9:28) up to Jesus' entry into Jerusalem (19:28), is a critical place to look for clues as to how to fix Church. In these ten chapters, Jesus is doing in-depth training with his disciples. Because these chapters lead us to the Passion story of Jesus' death and resurrection, they figure prominently in the scriptures we use during Lent (Year C, 2018). In them, Jesus teaches about the super-sized faith every churchgoer needs in order to be one of his active disciples. These lessons involve a measurable quantity that is best called *Spiritual Passion*.

For example, in Luke chapter 10, Jesus sends his disciples out on their second and most difficult training mission. We read:

> *After this the Lord appointed seventy-two others and sent them two by two ahead of him to every town and place where he was about to go. He told them, "The harvest is plentiful, but the workers are few. Ask the Lord of the harvest, therefore, to send out workers into his harvest field..." (vv 1-2)*
>
> *The seventy-two returned with joy and said, "Lord, even the demons submit to us in your name."*
>
> *[Jesus] replied, "I saw Satan fall like lightning from heaven. I have given you authority to trample on snakes and scorpions and to overcome all the power of the enemy; nothing will harm you. However, do not rejoice that the spirits submit to you, but rejoice that your names are written in heaven."*
>
> *At that time Jesus, full of joy through the Holy Spirit, said, "I praise you, Father, Lord of heaven and earth, because you have hidden these things from the wise and learned, and revealed them to little children. Yes, Father, for this is what you were pleased to do. (vv 17-21)*

Seventy-two is not very many people. The disciples had a lot of territory to cover in a short time. We might find ourselves identifying with the statement about too few people and too much work. Should Jesus have gathered more people before raising the bar of his expectations? No, because he knows that spiritual passion is not about having more people – nor is it a matter of finances, or having the "right" people in charge. It's not about having the right belief system, or a preacher who spouts fire and brimstone.

The disciples lack the basics at this point. They don't even understand that Jesus is going to die for their sins. Yet, two disciples on the road to a distant village can have enough spiritual passion to knock Satan off his seat. To raise spiritual passion, as individuals and as a fellowship of faith, we need to do four things:

1) CULTIVATE A SENSE OF *EXPECTATION* ABOUT PRAYER. At worship and in your small groups, take time to listen to people when they share how God is answering their prayers. How often do people get what they pray for? How does God transform their lives through their prayers? Take time in your church committees, not only to share prayer concerns, but speak about how prayer is working in your lives. When you pray, always ask, "What do I expect God to do with this prayer?" Keep a journal of prayers, their answers, and how your prayer life is changing. This is the same journey the disciples were on before they arrived at Luke chapter 10.

2) ALWAYS TRY TO LINK THE SCRIPTURE YOU ARE READING AND **hearing with how it is *Relevant* to daily life.** When scripture is read in church, the readers should tell how the passage connects to something they experienced in the past week. When you are studying the Bible, go beyond its historical context and meaning. Spend time talking about how it might influence the decisions you are making this week (See Fixing Church, chapter 6).

3) WITNESS WITH *JOY*. WHAT ABOUT YOUR FAITH MAKES YOU happy? What things in your church are you proud about? Nothing goes without saying. Think about that phrase. Until we put words to something, we aren't really committed to it. When people marry, they speak vows. We often confess our faith through historic texts such as the Apostle's Creed. We need to

learn how to express our current Joy. I suspect the disciples became effective witnesses for Jesus because when they showed up in each village, they were happy to talk about their faith. Discuss ways you as individuals can joyfully speak to those who aren't members of your church about Church (with a capital C). See Luke chapter 15 and how these three stories end in joy: verses 7, 9, and 32.

4) WORSHIP WITH *PASSION*. YOUR WORSHIP ON THE WEEKEND needs to be connected to your daily devotional life. There are so many things we need to do during that one hour a week. We can't become passionate about God with just that little bit of praise. The trick to worship is to make it a multiplier for what you do throughout the week. Each weekend we learn the songs, prayers, and uplifting truths that guide our daily worship. You need to design whatever daily worship works for you. Your church should be a helpful resource. Also, if you lead worship, think about how the individual pieces — the prayers, liturgy, hymns, and message — connect with the passion/emotional nature of the worship theme. If the subject is serious, then let the reflective nature of the content shine through. If the theme is joy, then be joyful. Bring appropriate passion to each segment of worship (See Fixing Church, chapter 5).

THE CHURCH'S FUEL

It helps to think of spiritual passion as a measurable quantity - like fuel in the church's gas tank. If you are honest, you can see in your mind's eye a gas gauge for your congregation's spirit. Are you full of the spirit or running on fumes? If you don't have much gas, you can't get very far. Churches with low spiritual passion limit their mission work. They say, "We have take care of ourselves first." But churches with high spiritual passion are marked by a spirit of generosity, saying, "You can't out-give God."

—

Spiritual Passion is the subject of my *Ezekiel's Bones* book, available through www.notperfectyet.com

FOR DISCUSSION

Discuss each of these questions. Then, see what Bill says. What insights did you have that Bill missed?
Be sure and talk about both what you are currently doing and what might be good for the future.

1) How is your church different from a social club (Elks, Masons, Kiwanis, etc.)?

2) What things have helped (or will help) your congregation to be as diverse as its neighborhood?

3) Life-threatening ills come to every congregation. There may be a financial crisis, a church conflict, or a time of poor leadership. What will help your church survive and serve God in the future?

BILL'S THOUGHTS:

1. Healthy Christian fellowships focus on their shared spiritual passion. People join a social club in order to be part of a group. Christian gatherings look more like social clubs when their emphasis is upon things other than a passionate love for God. Clubs can have good fellowship and do wonderful things, but anything they accomplish for God's kingdom is auxiliary. Churches must be different.

2. Real spiritual passion and diversity are interconnected. The secular world forms communities around shared interests (hence Facebook) and people who look similar. Church is different. Our shared passion for God forces us to recognize that we are all equal in Christ, and our humility makes us aware of the Holy Spirit's emphasis on diversity.

3. Churches live or die by their amount of spiritual passion. Churches don't close because they run out of members; rather, loss of meaning will kill any congregation. Unless your people understand prayer to be effective, scripture to be relevant, and witnessing to be their job – and unless they look forward to each week's worship because it inspires them deeply - they will flake off and join other fellowships.

3
BEING COMPASSIONATE

I once visited a church where the average age of the parishioners was 28, the music rocked, and instead of a choir they had a drama team. I was struck by how seriously Pastor Jim took Jesus' story of the Good Samaritan. Most people remember how a man on the road between Jericho and Jerusalem — where the temple is — gets beat up. But this young pastor emphasized how the priest and a Levite were in a hurry to get to church. They didn't stop to help the man who was beat up. This is typical church, with a small "c." People often think they are religious because they go to church. Because Pastor Jim had a congregation that wasn't in the habit of being religious, he was able to show them that being Church involves the big "C" of Compassion.

Compassion is all about loving people as Jesus did. Look at how Jesus spent his time:

- 24/7 he was helping his disciples become a loving fellowship.
- He spent most of his public ministry healing strangers and meeting their needs.

- He spent most of his teaching time trying to get everyone to be more compassionate.

When Jesus was giving his final instructions before going to the cross, he told his disciples:

> *As the Father has loved me, so have I loved you. Now remain in my love... My command is this: Love each other as I have loved you. Greater love has no one than this: to lay down one's life for one's friends.*
> - John 15:9, 12-13

The love that Jesus is talking about here travels in two directions. On the horizontal axis, it travels around the fellowship circle. The disciples are commanded to wash each other's feet, bear each other's burdens, and reinforce the love they feel for each other. This is the *lay down your life for your friends* concept. This horizontal axis leads us to form tight-knit church fellowships. The vertical axis is of equal importance. The upward goal is to love strangers and express our love for God by loving the world Jesus died for. We honor God by overcoming our prejudices and our natural shyness. By and large, Christians are amazingly cliquish people. Most of us are reluctant to connect new people to Jesus.

Jesus is clear that loving God by loving and serving new people is not optional. The Bible never tells us to go to a church building each week, sing three hymns, take an offering, and then listen to a sermon. Nowhere is churchgoing presented as a way to discharge our obligation to God. As we will see later in this book (chapter 5), genuine worship flows out of our love for God. This love, however, is meant to drive us outward in acts of compassion. We should never be seen passing by an opportunity to act compassionately. This is what separates the priest and the Levite from the Good Samaritan. The first two were in a hurry to go to church, with a little "c." The Good Samaritan was doing Church with a capital "C" (Luke 10:30-35).

Jesus dramatizes this vertical dimension in his last words to the disciples:

> ...go and make disciples of all nations, baptizing them in the name of the Father and of the Son and of the Holy Spirit, and teaching them to obey everything I have commanded you. And surely I am with you always, to the very end of the age.
> - Matthew 28:19-20

And,
> But you will receive power when the Holy Spirit comes on you; and you will be my witnesses in Jerusalem, and in all Judea and Samaria, and to the ends of the earth.
> - Acts 1:8

The disciples are literally looking up — this is the vertical dimension — as Jesus tells them to go wide, go far, and reach out to new people. He rises and returns to heaven. They go down off the mountain and into a world filled with strangers who don't know Jesus. The disciples must show their love for Jesus through their mission work and outreach to strangers.

Both the horizontal and the vertical dimensions of Jesus' love must always be on our hearts. Loving those we see in church each week helps us to grow as disciples of Christ. Christianity is intensely congregational. The religion of the Bible is all about people relating to each other in tight-knit fellowships (see chapter 4). That said, the purpose of our discipleship is to transform the world. We can't do what Jesus calls us to do and be shy, racist, bigoted, or *holier than thou*. We must be compassionate toward strangers. None of us are free to be one-hour-a-week Christians. Every gift that God has given us must be shared, especially with those who don't yet know God.

The central problem of church with a small "c" has been described this way:

> Church members in too many cases are like deep sea divers, encased in suits designed for many fathoms deep, marching bravely to pull out plugs in bath tubs.
> - From *Pastor's Postscript*, reprinted in <u>Mr. Jones, Meet the Master</u> by Peter Marshall

Week by week, most churches in the United States are getting smaller and becoming more trivial. The heyday of full pews and bursting Sunday school classrooms is now 60 years back in the rear view mirror (close to the time when Peter Marshall was chaplain to the Senate). The cause of this is not lack of resources, nor has the Holy Spirit stopped teaching Christians how to live their faith. We are well equipped in every way, but we would rather be a polite weekly gathering of friends than an intense, caring, fellowship. We would rather fix the stuck bathtub stoppers of our church buildings than be at work transforming the world.

MOVING IN BOTH DIRECTIONS

Each church must move energetically in both dimensions, vertical and horizontal. Imagine a church that spends all of its time and effort witnessing to those outside the church.

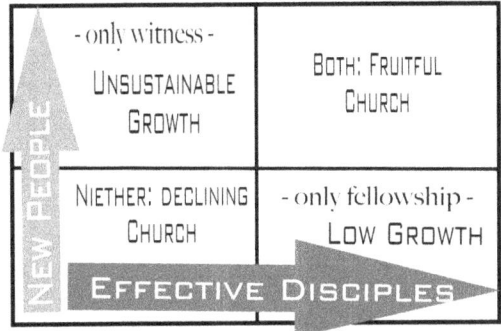

Its members are genuinely fulfilling Jesus' command to go unto all nations. They love others. They are constantly bringing new people into the church. They have the vertical dimension down pat. But too much emphasis in this direction leads to unsustainable growth. What goes up, may come down with a crash. The hard reality is that Christians need to have a healthy relationship with each other before they can witness to the world. It is by loving those in our fellowship that we become effective disciples for the transformation of the world.

After the Good Samaritan story, the next passage of scripture involves two sisters, Mary and Martha (Luke 10:38-42). Mary sits at Jesus' feet, surrounded by the familiar fellowship of his disciples. She is cultivating her own discipleship and learning about faith. Her sister, Martha, however, is busy elsewhere. When Martha complains about how lazy her sister is, Jesus doesn't take her side, because he realizes the importance of learning to be a disciple. That learning requires our sitting down with each other, forming small groups, and praying with each other; in short, it requires face-time. The inner circle of your church's fellowship needs to be deliberately developed.

BRING IT HOME...

Now consider your church. Are you simultaneously pursuing both arrows? If you fail to go forward in love in either dimension, your church will fall back into institutionalism. Love for the institution of the local church can easily replace both our love for new people and for the fellowship. If we stop being witnesses for Jesus, if we stop strengthening our discipleship and fellowship, then we become just like the priest and the Levite who pass by the man who had been beaten up by robbers.

This is Church: these two love-driven vectors. If this does not describe your church, then fix it.

Jesus wants us always to be compassionate. The whole focus of the church must be on nothing else. Every time we face a difficult decision, we must ask which path will force us to give more of ourselves to each other and to a world in need.

—-

For more, see http://billkemp.info/tags/compassion

FOR DISCUSSION

Discuss each of these questions. Then, see what Bill says. What insights did you have that Bill missed?
Be sure and talk about both what you are currently doing and what might be good for the future.

1) Is it possible for a church to be too generous, loving, and compassionate toward strangers? Should we intentionally reach out to those who may never darken the door of our church?

2) Is it possible for a church to be too serious about building a healthy fellowship? Is it important that all members of your church become the best disciples for Jesus Christ that they can be?

3) Has your church become too "institutional"? Instead of being concerned about reaching new people or developing a deeper fellowship, are you simply concerned with nickels and noses (the money in the offering plate and the number of people in the pews)?

Bill's thoughts:

1) Jesus' love never came with any strings attached. People know when we are interested in them only because we want them to join our church and help us pay the bills. Remember, the "Church exists by mission, just as fire exists by burning."

2) People can have either a surface relationship with Jesus, or they can become real disciples. A church can have a "little dab will do you" approach to faith, or it can constantly encourage its members to go deeper. This means committing ourselves to relating together in small groups, studying together, and being genuinely concerned about each other. In addition, it

involves discovering ways to serve our community by working together as teams of disciples.

3) IF YOUR CHURCH WERE TO RECEIVE A SUDDEN WINDFALL OF $10,000, would the money be used for something institutional or something missional? Would the money serve the interests of the congregation's current members, or would it go for discipleship training and reaching out to new people? (I know, I am answering a question with a question).

4
BEING A FELLOWSHIP

Because of my travel schedule, I am in my home church only about one Sunday in three. Even though I have been attending this same congregation for seven years, I know only about half the people. I am what bird-watchers call an irregular. To make matters worse, when I miss church, I attend the Internet. I have found a worship service that is uploaded as a podcast by a first class church. The music suits me and the preaching is way above average. Also, I live where the weather can make going to my local church a chore. The question is:

Why should I maintain any relationship with the church in my neighborhood?

My answer is that Jesus designed Christianity to be congregational. Our faith functions best when we are committed members of an intimate fellowship. A local church can be fine if it has a good preacher, an on-tune choir, and plenty of activities for the children, but it can't be Church with a capital "C" without getting personal. Church has to care about us and provide us with a supportive fellowship. Grapes are found in clusters, sheep in flocks, and bananas in bunches. We live out our individual Christianity within a local church.

JESUS ON FELLOWSHIP

When Jesus says, "I am the vine; you are the branches," he is implying that we will be clustered in church-sized groups (John 15:1-8). When he says "I am the good shepherd," he is emphasizing the relational aspect of Christian life that gathers us into flocks. I may feel inspired when I put on my headphones and listen to a worship service podcast, but this is not the religious life Jesus planned for his disciples. We get it wrong when we say, "I go to church for the message," or worse still, "I go to church because its what I've always done on Sundays." Getting it right involves seeing Church as a fellowship that we enter into, contributing not just our money, but ourselves. Relationship breeds discipleship. Who we are when we get together as Christians determines who we will be when we go out into the world as Jesus' disciples.

When you think about it, Jesus doesn't speak about church the way we do. Most people think of church as a physical place. For those on the council, church is a building that must be maintained. For those of us in other areas of leadership, church is a set of programs that we must organize week after week, year after year. For many, church is a club that we want more people to join. But Jesus never speaks about his ministry needing a physical location. He never uses the word "church" to mean a building with a steeple and at least two offering plates.

ECCLESIA = CHURCH

In the Bible, the word "church" doesn't appear until the New Testament. I always tell people that Jesus invented Church, but that is only partly true. There have always been assemblies or gatherings for religious purposes. In Matthew 16:18, Peter (nicknamed *Rock*) confesses his conviction that Jesus is both God's son and the expected messiah. Jesus then tells his disciples that this *rock* (or faith) will be the foundation of his "Church" (we don't know if he used air quotes). Then later, in Matthew 18:15-17, Jesus outlines a process for correcting misbehaving believers. When all else fails, we are to gather the whole church (or *ecclesia,* the common Greek word for an assembly) to decide what to do.

Jesus doesn't use the word "church" again until 60 years later when he comes in a vision to John on Patmos Island (Revelation 1:4-3:22). Here church has become Church. Jesus sends a personal message to each of seven fellowships. He calls them by name, treating each Church as a living being. Each Church, in spite of its faults, is a sacred thing. Each assembly has a soul (see chapter 7). It is unlikely that any of these groups owned a building. Persecution will soon scatter many of them from their homes and make them refugees. Yet, a candle burns before the throne of God in honor of each of these Churches. Jesus constantly intercedes on their behalf, and I believe he does the same for your Church.

BETTER TOGETHER?

Church is a classic case of the whole being greater than the sum of the parts. We use the word "family" to describe the relational character of our assembly. Families can be large or small — their value is unrelated to their size. They can be housed in mansions or scattered in humble dwellings across the landscape. They can even be homeless. Churches, too, can exist without buildings. They can meet in coffee shops, jail cells, and senior citizen high-rises.

To carry the analogy one step further, churches, like families, can be healthy or dysfunctional. This is critical. The assembly of believers can be a safe place where we relate to each other in Christian love, or it can be a pit of vipers. Some congregations put the "fun" in "dysfunctional." As I visit various congregations, I am reminded of the opening line of *Anna Karenina:*

> *Happy families are all alike; every unhappy family is unhappy in its own way.*
> - Leo Tolstoy

Go back to the two arrow illustration in chapter 3. This is the portrait of every happy church: energy moving upward and outward. There is a commitment to seek new people, matched by a willingness to intensely love those within the fellowship and form them into effective disciples. Happy churches do these two things. They do them when the roof is leaking and when the sun is shining. When they have a great pastor, and when they have a lemon. Every happy church is the same.

Every unhappy church has its own set of woes. It may have a great pastor, but not enough money in the offering plate to keep her for long. It may have an endowment fund to take care of its building, but nobody interested in being on the mission or evangelism committee. It may be plum in the middle of a neighborhood littered with children, but absolutely clueless about how to get them into Sunday school.

Fixing the unhappy church is a matter of changing the whole system, curing the whole fellowship. There is no simple solution that fits every congregation. Remember, when our family is unhappy, we are each dysfunctional in our own way. Looking over at the neighboring church and saying, "Let's do what they're doing," won't help you. Also, be aware that if there were a simple solution to finding happiness, you would have tried it already.

Many people go to therapy these days. People who struggle with Post Traumatic Stress Disorder, grief, addiction, etc., will make time in their schedule to participate in group therapy. Often, dysfunctional families will get help from a counselor who specializes in treating the whole family system. If your congregation were to enter into therapy, what would it look like?

Today, a number of consultants and non-profit agencies work in a therapeutic fashion with local churches. In most denominations, you can also find ministers who, like myself, have been trained to act as transitional guides. Whether or not you ask an outsider to help your congregation, it is useful to declare a "Transitional Period." During that three-to-eighteen-month period, focus on communication. Learn to listen to each other. At the beginning of each gathering and committee meeting, allow time for honest discussion. Yield the floor to people who don't usually speak. If you have a mission statement, dust it off. Look at whether it incorporates the two arrows, reaching new people and developing a caring fellowship. Is it just words on a page or does it challenge us to be disciples of Jesus Christ?

During any transitional period, there is a rule:

Developing the right process for making a decision is more important than any one decision.

This goes along with the saying, "The ends never justify the means." When families, congregations, and political entities become dysfunctional, they tend to fight about trivial things. Unhappy churches throw away their processes for making good decisions. They lose their wisdom as a group, because they are too swayed by individuals trying to get their own way. Wisdom is only found by seeking her. To find wisdom, we must decide that the process is more important than any one result.

RULES FOR A HEALTHY FELLOWSHIP

We all know that we should do unto others as we would wish them to do for us (Matthew 7:12). In building fellowship, we flesh out the *Golden Rule* in three ways:

1) SEEK DIVERSITY. STOP TRYING TO GET MORE "PEOPLE LIKE US" into your church. Don't play to your base, as they say in the competitive world of politics. Practice accepting strangers where they are, as they are. Intentionally try to understand those outside your walls. If you can learn to love the nonbeliever and/or alien, then God will also teach you how to love those currently in your fellowship.

2) SEEK INPUT FROM THOSE WHO AREN'T CURRENTLY AT THE table. In every church, there are people who are not consulted when decisions are made. A church may publicize its meetings with an open invitation, but the agenda isn't shared, the financial statements aren't posted, and the person in the pew is clueless as to what is going on behind closed doors. We may nominate a new member to a committee, but when they show up, their opinion is never sought. Congregations rarely take the

time to seek input from those not in charge, or survey the church's neighbors, or to consider the needs of the transient (irregular birds) of the community. Yet, this is where Jesus did his ministry.

3) GIVE PEOPLE THE OPPORTUNITY TO FAIL. PERFECTIONISM IS ONE of the most deadly diseases afflicting the church today. We are not willing to try new things because we are afraid of failure and the criticism of those who have always done things their way. The only perfection to which Jesus calls us is perfection in love.

> Nothing in the Golden Rule says that others will treat us as we have treated them. It only says that we must treat others in a way that we would want to be treated.
> - Rosa Parks

Using a therapeutic model to fix the local church is the subject of my *The Church Transition Workbook: Getting Your Church in Gear*, available through www.notperfectyet.com

FOR DISCUSSION

Discuss each of these questions. Then, see what Bill says. What insights did you have that Bill missed?
Be sure and talk about both what you are currently doing and what might be good for the future.

1) IS IT POSSIBLE TO BE A CHRISTIAN WITHOUT BEING PART OF A church?

2) MARTIN LUTHER KING FAMOUSLY SAID THAT THE SUNDAY morning worship time is the most segregated hour of the week. Would we have fewer problems with racism and income inequality in America if our churches were more diverse?

3) ON A SCALE FROM ONE TO TEN, WITH TEN BEING GREAT, HOW well do you treat those who are new to your fellowship?

BILL'S THOUGHTS:

1) Today the word "Christian" is used to distinguish our form of religion from those propounded by the world's other religions. In the beginning, though, "Christian" meant someone who belonged to a fellowship of people united by their faith in their living lord, Jesus Christ (see Acts 11:25-26).

2) RELIGION IS OFTEN USED TO REINFORCE OUR PREJUDICES. IN Nazi Germany, for example, religious symbols were used to indoctrinate a people in hatred. This is the opposite of what Jesus taught: he made his disciples walk across the bad neighborhoods of Samaria. He accepted invitations to eat with outcasts and people who were considered sinful by the religious leaders of his day. We follow him by intentionally befriending and inviting into our fellowship those who are different from us.

3) Most churches are like a loaf of French bread; hard and crusty on the outside, soft and moist once you make it within. We sometimes require people to learn our jargon, come every Sunday for years, and marry our daughters, before we consider them a real part of our fellowship. It is only by recognizing the problem that we become less of an isolated clique.

5
BEING WORSHIP-FILLED

The military services have rules that prohibit their soldiers from *public displays of affection* (PDA), such as holding hands or kissing, while in uniform. The reason for this is simple. The uniform reminds soldiers that they are professionals. In uniform, they live by a different code than we civilians. Their on duty actions may include the use of deadly force. A kiss, or even holding your spouse's hand, disrupts this image. Worship disrupts what has become uniform in our lives. The Call to Worship invites us take on a different mantle. We enter a place where it is perfectly okay to speak about our love for God, to sing him a kiss with our hymns, to hold His hand at the altar rail.

It is by retreating to this sanctuary with its acceptance of PDAs in that we undo our training in selfishness. Worship should cause us to question the competitive mindset of our daily grind. Worship should make us more compassionate. It should shift our perspective so that we see things from God's point of view. PDAs play a role in this. They allow us to put on the clothing of righteousness.

We are not required to attend worship, any more than a

married couple is required to publicly display their affection for each other. But why does a wedding service always end with a kiss? Is not this act a kind of *fix*? We know intuitively that when we display affection, our relationships are improved. There are limits, but what is important to us in our heart has to make it into the market place. Public and private reinforce each other. In the same way, our weekend worship of God ought to strengthen our daily devotion, while our personal prayer time greatly benefits the life of our church.

We all tend to like what we like. The dedicated choir member judges the worship service on the quality of the music. The preacher thinks that worship happened this week because a number of people complimented the sermon. The extrovert likes the greeting time, while new parents like the children's message. Task-oriented people like worship to be done on time so they can check "church" off their list for the week. Some think that church should be to worship as a microwave is to food. What we like about a worship service may have little to do with how effective that time has been for helping a random group of people become Church.

HOW DO WE FEEL ABOUT GOD?

So let me put it simply. Worship has a lot to do with how we feel about God. It is tied through PDAs to the emotional component of our faith. When we face a challenge at work on Monday, or hear bad news on Thursday, we want the comfort provided by our church the previous week to support our prayer life. We also want to be uplifted by the joy we felt when we worshiped. The heart is at the center of our bodies; so should it be at the center of our worship. It is good to have a theological or rational takeaway from the service, but the substance of our worship is emotional.

Love the Lord your God with all your heart and with all your soul and with all your mind.
- Matthew 22:37 and Deuteronomy 6:5

ABOUT HEART AND MIND, WE SHOULD SAY TWO THINGS:

First, that appropriate public display of affection for God is predetermined by the congregation's culture. In some churches, the volume setting is much higher than in others. This doesn't mean that those who roll in the aisle are more religious than those who spend time in silent reflection. The American religious experience runs the gamut from snake-handling Pentecostals to stoic New England Quakers. Each congregation positions itself somewhere on that continuum. Moving left or right doesn't make your worship better or worse; it only makes it fit a different subset of Christians. Our worship is kept honest when it resonates with our emotional needs in a way that is appropriate to our congregational culture.

Second, to make worship work, each component must carry the appropriate emotional tone. The Apostle Paul writes, "Rejoice with those who rejoice; mourn with those who mourn" (Romans 12:15), and, "If one part suffers, every part suffers with it; if one part is honored, every part rejoices with it. Now you are the body of Christ, and each one of you is a part of it" (I Corinthians 12:26-27). When we come to worship, we enter into a journey together. Sometimes we sing a hymn about the glories of Heaven, our final destination. Then it is appropriate that the music makes us feel joyful. Sometimes we are joined together in prayer for the burdens borne by our fellow travelers. Then our earnest love for each other may be best expressed quietly. If the content of the scripture passages and message involves a rational decision to change our behavior, then the emotional tone should be palpably more contrite. If the children of Israel are crossing the Jordan River, I want to know that it is chilly. I also want to go home with a gut-level awareness that life's obstacles can chill the body but not the soul.

EMOTIONAL TONE

All those involved with worship leadership should look at how their piece fits in with the whole. Is there an overall theme for this week that sets the tone? How should the congregation feel when they experience this part? If it is a scripture lesson, how can I prepare people to hear it? If it is a narrative about God's people being saved from disaster, for example, how can I help people understand the dilemma? What should my tone of voice be at each line? Should I choose a different translation? Fixing worship takes preparation. It is a team effort. It begins with clear communication between each of the people involved in leadership.

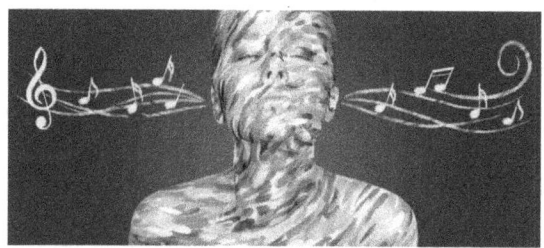

CONTEMPORARY MUSIC

Every congregation today has some anxiety about whether their music is relevant to the people they hope to reach and bring into church. I saw a cartoon a while back in which the Devil was rejoicing because a bagpiper had died and been sent below, implying that bagpipes provide the music of Hell. I know church leaders who believe that contemporary Christian music is of the Devil, while others adamantly believe the opposite. They are all wrong. We "know" from world history that the music of Hell is Beethoven, Strauss, and Richard Wagner. When the Nazis came to power, they took over the operas of Wagner, the marches of Strauss, and rejoiced in the Germanness of Beethoven's music. In fact, Wagner had been dead for 50 years; Strauss parted ways from the Nazis in 1935, and the long-dead Beethoven, who had been famously un-political, stated that "strength is the morality of the man who stands out from the rest."

Music carries emotional freight, sometimes in unintended ways. I have heard people complain that when they sing repetitious choruses, they feel patronized. Faith has been "dumbed down" for them. Others, hearing the regular chord structure and meter of traditional hymns, feel that the faith spoken of in this music is old, dead, and irrelevant to today's high-tech world. When music doesn't connect with a congregation's culture, it just feels bad. When music is chosen because it suits the tastes of one or two leaders, it rarely travels home with the congregation. It is vitally important that our worship music carry our faith throughout the week ahead.

To this end, those who want to fix church must be aware of who's attending. One style of music isn't better or worse than another; neither is one order or worship more godly than another. Worship that works is finely tuned to the congregation's culture. Some churches in Texas have cowboy worship with the appropriate country music. On the other hand, a packed congregation in downtown Houston prides itself in having a traditional liturgy that would make John Wesley (1703 - 1791) happy. Some congregations offer Taizé worship, where silence is prominent, the liturgy chanted, preaching absent, and the songs beautifully simple. Others offer an "early bird" worship where the music is prerecorded, the leadership casual, and the focus is on prayer and the availability of holy communion.

If you are sensitive to others' worship needs, you will notice divisions in your congregational culture. A significant number of people just may not be connecting with the worship service you offer. You may also notice that the culture of the unchurched people near your location merits praying to consider whether God wants you to start a worship service geared for them. Whenever a congregation adds a worship service with a different feel, there is always backlash. Yes, for a while the fellowship will be divided, as people sort themselves out and decide which worship works for them. The "new people" dimension of Christian discipleship (see chapter 3) requires us to move beyond our comfort zone.

WORSHIP AND SPIRITUAL PASSION

Worship must do whatever will build spiritual passion (see chapter 2). It may not be necessary for an ordained pastor to bring a sermon, but holy scripture does need to be presented in such a way that encourages people to see its relevance in their lives. A specific order of worship is not mandated, but prayer must be taught and practiced, so the newcomer understands it and prays expectantly. Prayer must be held accountable for results. Worship witnesses with joy when there is a welcoming spirit. Worship is inspiring when it connects with our emotions and leads us to publicly display our affection for God. In return, God often expresses His love for us during our worship.

Finally, invite people to enjoy the sacraments. In churches that need fixing, the sacraments are viewed as an obligation, to be dealt with as quickly and rigidly as possible. Congregations that have Church, however, recognize that the bread and the cup are gifts from God; consequently, communion is celebrated with a richness and a genuine spirit of worship. Holy Thursday is one of the most important services of the year. I have been fortunate to serve several churches that practiced weekly communion. Every week I would look at the scriptures, pondering how they connected to communion, and I was never disappointed. Communion is one of the languages God uses to speak to our hearts.

FOR DISCUSSION

Discuss each of these questions. Then, see what Bill says. What insights did you have that Bill missed?
Be sure and talk about both what you are currently doing and what might be good for the future.

1) ARE YOU AS AN INDIVIDUAL COMFORTABLE WITH THINKING OF worship as a public display of your affection for God?

2) WORSHIP MUST INVITE PEOPLE TO SEE SCRIPTURE AS RELEVANT to their lives, and prayer as effective today. Does your church participation encourage your daily devotional life?

3) WHICH OF JESUS' BEATITUDES (MATTHEW 5:3-10, SEE CHAPTER 1) deserves special emphasis during your congregation's worship?

BILL'S INSIGHTS:

1) If a congregation increases its Spiritual Passion (chapter 2), the worship service will "catch fire." The presence of the Holy Spirit always transforms worship into a public display of our love for God.

2) Every church has Bible readings and prayer. Few churches are intentional about making the readings relevant and the prayers effective.

3) We begin anew each week with two kinds of people in worship: those who need to hear that Jesus is blessing them today, and those who need to learn how to bless their neighbor with the love of God.

BEING BIBLICAL

Jesus says that people who understand his words and put them into practice become like a house built on a good foundation. The storms of life assail this rock, but the house remains secure (Matthew 7:24-27). How can we hope to experience this promise if we don't know Jesus' words? Most people, even most church-going-faithful-every-Sunday Christians, make a lot of assumptions about what Jesus said. They think they know what he meant to say, even though they don't remember more than a few trite phrases. One churchgoer in a hundred actually tries to put into practice what he reads in the New Testament.

IN THE MIDDLE OF THE OLD TESTAMENT WE READ:

> The law of the Lord is perfect,
> refreshing the soul.
> The statutes of the Lord are trustworthy,
> making wise the simple.
> The precepts of the Lord are right,

> giving joy to the heart.
> The commands of the Lord are radiant,
> giving light to the eyes.
> The fear of the Lord is pure,
> enduring forever.
> The decrees of the Lord are firm,
> and all of them are righteous.
> They are more precious than gold,
> than much pure gold;
> they are sweeter than honey,
> than honey from the honeycomb.
> By them your servant is warned;
> in keeping them there is great reward.
> - Psalm 19:7-11

Seems a bit extreme, right? The Bible tastes better than baklava (v.10). It refreshes our soul, keeps us from having to remain stupid (v.7) and from making dumb mistakes (v.11). It makes us joyful (v.8). If these claims are true, why are so few people enthusiastic about daily devotions? Why do so few sign up for small group Bible studies?

> Success is like a snowball... it takes momentum to build.
> – Steve Ferrante (a marketing guru)

THE SNOWBALL EFFECng

In many areas of life, the snowball effect reigns. When you have just a scattering of people reading the Bible, they are like a thin coating of frost on the grass. Their passion for God is barely noticed by others. When attendance at study groups in church is spotty, those that do come doubt the importance of what they are doing. But make small group participation and home Bible study a key priority in the church, and soon there will be enough snow on the ground to form a snowball. People will begin to encourage each other to know their Bible. Then this bible-thing picks up momentum as the snowball rolls downhill, getting bigger and bigger. We see the same thing happening in the secular world with hit songs, movies, and Jim Patterson books. Why can't this happen with the Bible in your church? Perhaps the greatest asset a congregation can have is biblical literacy.

Human beings are herd animals. We take on new behaviors because we see others doing the same thing. Some churches hold "Read the Bible in a Year" contests and honor those who are successful in their commitment. Other churches make church membership dependent upon participating in a small group or Sunday School class. Church leaders should be asked to speak about their devotional habits. What we say publicly about the Bible matters. Reading the Bible can only become a common practice if those of us who do it are willing to say how sweet it is and how it has changed our lives.

Bible reading is not just like a snowball gaining momentum as it goes downhill. It is like an avalanche disrupting everything in its path. Biblical literacy often precedes periods of congregational growth, as well as times of national spiritual revival. The great reformer Martin Luther said:

> The Bible is alive, it speaks to me; it has feet, it runs after me; it has hands, it lays hold of me.
> - Table Talk

These words did not sound crazy within the context of the great spiritual revival of the 16th century. It is hard to imagine the Protestant Reformation taking hold without Gutenberg's invention of the printing press and the ready availability of Bibles in the common language of the people. If a heavy, expensive, print-only edition of God's word can be alive and chase after Mr. Luther, what effect can our smart phone Bible apps and easily portable Christian ebooks have on us?

BIBLE-READING PASSION

Back in chapter 2 we began to ponder the nature of spiritual passion. The relevance of the Bible to the daily life of the person in the pew is directly related to the congregation's level of spiritual passion. People don't have to believe that the Bible is infallible, or all be reading the same version. They only need to be open to the Bible's wisdom and allow this living thing to become a daily guide.

People often complain that the Bible is complicated, inaccessible, and fit only for preachers to read. This may be true of some parts when taken out of context. If I had never seen a horse, but only a hoof preserved in a bottle of formaldehyde, I would assume that the horse is one ugly critter. The same often happens to people who begin to read the Bible in the wrong place, or worse yet, encounter it only when it is broken up into little bits, read poorly in church. To taste the sweetness of the Bible, you need to read it with a sense of context. A bit of background has to be communicated to us about old King Hezekiah and the problems facing him, before we can see any reason to care that he watched the shadow on the palace stairs go back ten steps (Isaiah 38). So we may need a teacher to get us into the Bible; fortunately, today we all have the Internet and numerous Bible translations with commentary and footnotes.

But that said, the Bible needs to be read prayerfully. I believe that the Holy Spirit waits to unlock it for each of us. When we approach God's word with humble hearts and an open spirit, we are always satisfied. This is especially true when we study with other people. A small group, or even one other person, multiplies our capacity to comprehend and find words that are relevant to our lives. Regarding interpreting the Bible, this promise is true:

> If any of you lacks wisdom, you should ask God, who gives generously to all...
> - James 1:5a

While the Bible has some ugly bits (I am no fan of II Samuel 20:9, for example), it has a central core that is life-changing and indispensable. The Passion Story, found in Mark chapters 14 through 16, lays the foundation both for our individual lives as Christians, and for our life together as Church. We read how Jesus enters Jerusalem, has his last supper with his disciples, is arrested, tried, crucified and buried. Then we are confronted with an empty tomb and the reality that Jesus has conquered death. The writing here is fast-paced, more thrilling than a John Grisham novel. The reading is easy. The message, however, is deep. A child can grasp its truth, but it takes a lifetime to explore its meaning.

SEASONS OF THE SPIRIT

Fixing our church requires us to both reclaim the Bible's relevance and restore the role of the Passion Story in the church's calendar, worship, and study. The practice of giving things up for Lent never had any scriptural support, but it brought the liturgical calendar, with its focus on Jesus' passion, into the daily experience of the faithful for that forty-day period. Putting on special dramas and musical events for Holy Week also helps to tell the story. Families should set aside time for planning their

Lent and Holy week celebrations each year. They may want to have a soup meal each week in which they read and discuss together part of the Passion Story. Church leaders should have special team meeting to plan how to maximize the worship experience for these seven weeks. Advertising and church outreach should be intensified during this season.

Everything we do in church is related to those seven days. We are people of the cross. We come with the disciples to this sacred moment when God gives his only son that we should not perish but have eternal life. The rest of the New Testament flows out of that moment, and the church is born with the single task of witnessing to it. As we renew our commitment to read the Bible, we also pledge to make the story of Jesus on the cross central to our daily lives. What would it take for you to become an expert on this story?

FOR DISCUSSION

Discuss each of these questions. Then, see what Bill says. What insights did you have that Bill missed?
Be sure and talk about both what you are currently doing and what might be good for the future.

1). Yes, but how? What specific things should your church do in order to encourage biblical literacy?

2) Have you ever actually changed your behavior because of something you read in the Bible?

3) What would it take for you to experience the Passion Story and Holy Week in a new way this year? What should the church add to its Lenten schedule?

BILL'S INSIGHTS:

1) Your church needs a strategy for getting the Bible into each parishioner's hands. You can purchase cheap paperback versions from www.Zondervan.com, put links in your bulletin for ebooks and apps, and publicize the free web-bible at www.biblegateway.com . You should have an overlapping strategy for encouraging bible reading among children, youth, and adults.

2) This is a question that is best asked every week, or perhaps every day. Find a Christian saint whom you trust and ask how the Bible has changed her life.

3) Now is the time to plan for next year. Lent and Advent are when the church has the greatest opportunity to reach those without a church home. Many churches do outreach before Christmas; few put the same effort into telling the Passion story.

WRITE DOWN YOUR IDEAS REGARDING PROMOTING THE PASSION STORY IN YOUR CHURCH AND THE SURROUNDING COMMUNITY:

Extra Credit: Think ahead for the next two to three years

BEING CHURCH (SOUL)

In the long run, we cannot fix our church without saving our own soul. Each of these seven lessons demonstrates a connection between the faith we practice as individuals and the faith we share as a church. We can do Church only by changing ourselves. The prerequisite for a great church is a broken, prayerful, and intentionally godly people. We care for the soul of our local church by caring for our own soul.

THE WORD "SOUL" REMINDS US OF TWO THINGS:

First, that our current life on this earth is but a small segment of a much greater eternal life that we will continue to enjoy after this.

Second, that what lies within us is more important than anything external. Our bodies may be failing, but our immortal soul shines ever brighter (see II Corinthians 4:7-12). Our pockets may be empty and shoes worn through, but we are rich in the things that matter.

It is important that we not think of our soul as a little wispy cloud that gets "saved" and flies to heaven when we die. Our soul is the spiritual core upon which we depend every day, so that we might live as disciples of Jesus Christ. Each of us has been loved by God into his Church for a reason. The Apostle Paul writes:

> ...*continue to work out your salvation with fear and trembling, for it is God who works in you to will and to act in order to fulfill his good purpose.*
> -Philippians 2:12b

In the mid-1700s, John Wesley organized the movement that would later become the United Methodist Church. When he sent the his first ministers to America. he said, "You have nothing to do except save souls." That is still pretty good advice to those who seek to fix church today. You must be always mindful that doing Church is related to the larger part of our lives that goes on after we leave this earth. When we take communion, we celebrate the heavenly banquet. We look back to the evening when Jesus explained to his disciples that he was going to the cross so they might feast in heaven with him. We look at the people in the pews beside us and we know that we will enjoy this fellowship forever. A saved soul becomes something to rejoice in when you do Church.

The word "soul" also reminds us that we are disciples of Jesus Christ. We continue to work out our salvation by telling others that they are loved by God, and also by feeding the hungry, bringing water to the thirsty, providing clothing and shelter to the refugee, caring for the sick or imprisoned, etc. (Matthew 25:31-46). This is what it means to be a disciple of Jesus Christ.

When John Wesley said, "You have nothing to do except save souls," he was excluding from the priority list a lot of what today's churches consider essential. Neither Wesley nor Jesus said a word about building maintenance or the annual stewardship drive. Churches that focus on saving souls take a very functional approach to their buildings and finances. If the building enables them to be in mission to the neighborhood, then they invest in it. If the expenditures supported by the church budget help people to be more passionate about God and to be better disciples in this world, then Church is good for the soul and we don't mind giving passionately toward it.

If Jesus had done nothing on earth except save our souls, it would be enough. Perhaps that is a better way to understand his work. He was able to complete his earthly ministry in three years and give the gift of his life on the cross in three hours because he cared about nothing but our souls. Remember this the next time you complain that there isn't enough time to do what you want. Perhaps your desires are in the wrong place. I find myself pondering Jesus' words to Martha, the patron saint of all church committee workers:

> Martha, Martha. You are worried and upset about many things, but few things are needed—or indeed only one.
> - Luke 10:41-42a

The one thing Mary sought when she sat at Jesus' feet was nourishment for her soul. It is helpful to define the word "soul" very broadly. Heart and soul are often used together to speak about the internal quality of our lives. Our soul makes us human; while it is a mysterious entity, it is plainly connected to the unique purpose God has for each of us. We express our own souls through what and whom we choose to love. Conversely, when we love the wrong things and worship idols, we damage our souls. When we live according to the prayer Jesus taught us, trusting God for our daily bread, displaying forgiveness in our relationships, allowing the Holy Spirit to guide us away from temptation, and expecting God's kingdom to be manifested in our world, then we live soul-fully.

OUTWARD AND UPWARD

As individual Christians, our focus on soul pushes us outward and upward. We see this current life, with all of its overwhelming burdens and petty problems, in the light of the larger life our soul has in God. A hundred years from now, we will still be alive. From our soul's perch in heaven, few of our current obsessions will matter. Feeding our soul shifts our vision upward, freeing us to do discipleship and minister to the needs of others. Our vision shifts outward.

I believe that each local church also has a soul. When church leaders pay attention to the soul of their fellowship, their hopes for Church shift upward and outward. The pettiness of congregations is legendary. For every Mary in the church, there are a hundred Marthas. For every visionary Isaiah or John, there are a hundred doubting Thomases. So we must keep reminding ourselves that we have nothing to do but save souls.

This leads us to a sense of urgency. Every time we gather for worship, the focus of what we say and do is either upward and outward or inward and downward. Every time a church committee meets, regardless of its agenda, the consequence of its decisions moves the church one notch upward and outward, or it shifts the focus inward and downward.

Think of a tornado rumbling across the prairie. It encounters a cow. Now if Bessie Mae is picked upward, she is unlikely to be dropped down in the same field; the forces that carry her up will also carry her outward. Churches are unable to go upward — in finances, membership, spiritual growth, etc. — without going outward in acts of compassion for their neighbors.

God has designed Church to be on particular kind of spiral staircase: we can't go up without going out. If we continue to be concerned mostly with our own stuff, be that the color of the carpet in the narthex or the amount we should pay our pastor, then we will only descend. Even with the best intentions and hard work, if most of our actions are aimed only at making our own people happy, we will shrink like a black hole, until we become a selfish singularity.

This is what I have come to call the Spiral Rule; it applies to every congregation, has no exceptions, and goes back to Jesus (Luke 6:38). The rule is: *Churches that face outward go upward; congregations that focus inward shrink downward until they become a selfish singularity.*

—

More about the Spiral Rule can be found in Reality Check 101, chapter 6.

FOR DISCUSSION

*Discuss each of these questions. Then, see what Bill says. What insights did you have that Bill missed?
Be sure and talk about both what you are currently doing and what might be good for the future.*

1) Do you agree that your local church has a soul? What makes your congregation distinct from the other religious organizations in your community?

2) Jesus says, "Give, and it will be given to you. A good measure, pressed down, shaken together and running over, will be poured into your lap. For with the measure you use, it will be measured to you" (Luke 6:38). Do you think this applies to your church's giving toward outreach and missions?

3) Recall one recent decision that you, or a committee you were on, made on behalf of the church. Using the Spiral Rule, do you think it took you inward and downward, or upward and outward?

BILL'S INSIGHTS:

1) Christianity is fundamentally congregational. Each congregation is an organic, living thing. For most parishioners, the lifespan of their church is much greater than their own time on earth. The church came into existence before we arrived, and we

hope it will continue after we are gone. It has a soul that is broader than our own. It will nurture a variety of people. It has its own faith and culture. Like the seven churches of Revelation, it has a place before the throne of God.

2) GENEROSITY IS ESSENTIAL FOR CHURCH.

3) THE SPIRAL RULE HAS A LOT TO DO WITH HOW WE BEGAN THIS study. In chapter 1, we saw Jesus going outside the walls of the established religion. He met with people who felt rejected by God. By teaching the Beatitudes (Matthew 5:1-11), he worked to fix the downward and inward practices of their religious leaders.

4) WHAT DID YOU THINK OF THIS FIXING CHURCH 7.0?

You can also leave a comment or send your review to contact@billkemp.info

EBOOK READERS HAVE THE FOLLOWING QUICK LINKS:
For comments using an **Airtable** *survey.*
For e-letter signup through **MailChimp.**
Thanks,
- Bill Kemp

ABOUT THE AUTHOR & HIS BOOKS

Bill is an ordained clergy person in the Western Pennsylvania Conference of the United Methodist Church, and an unofficial instigator for change. After serving a variety of local churches for 31 years, he switched into full time writing in 2010. Now he divides his time between nonfiction (books for churches and individuals going through transition) and creative fiction. His second novel, **Mary Sees All** - *the Race to Save Jesus from the Cross*, will be released May 5, 2018. He is the author of nine other books.

Bill also does workshops and consulting (see www.notperfectyet.com). He maintains a blog at www.billkemp.info where he posts each Tuesday about the upcoming scriptures (lectionary), as well as, addresses topics related to church management, social justice, and personal transition. Lately his creative work has extended into image production, media design, and drama.

The book business has changed drastically since 2004 when Bill Kemp was first published by his denomination's press, Discipleship Resources (The United Methodist Church). While traditional houses still provide needed resources for local churches and a platform for popular authors, Bill launched **Not Perfect Yet Publishing** with an eye to providing a more "unvarnished" guide to church life, contemporary issued, and personal spirituality. He appreciates your feed back (contact@billkemp.info).

For more:

www.notperfectyet.com
contact@billkemp.info

ALSO BY BILL KEMP:

Reality Check 101: *New Paths for a Changing Church*

The Church Transition Workbook : *Getting Your Church in Gear*

Holy Places, Small Spaces: *A Hopeful Future for the Small Membership Church*

Ezekiel's Bones: *Rekindling Your Congregation's Spiritual Passion*

David's Harp: *Returning Harmony to Conflicted Congregations*

Saul's Armor: *Reforming Your Building and Organization for Ministry*

Jesus' New Command: *Rediscovering the Joy of Fellowship*

Jonah's Whale: *Reconnecting the Congregation with Mission*

Peter's Boat: *Renewing the Vitality of Burned-out Church Workers*

Going Home: *Facing Life's Final Moments Without Fear* - cowritten with **Diane Kerner Arnett**

Coming May 2018: Mary Sees All - *a novel about the Race to save Jesus from the Cross.*

Books can be purchased at www.amazon.com/author/billkemp

- Or -

Ordered Bill's webpage www.notperfectyet.com

Bill's blog can be found at www.billkemp.info

www.ingramcontent.com/pod-product-compliance
Lightning Source LLC
Chambersburg PA
CBHW070551300426
44113CB00011B/1862